Conte

Step 1: **CHANGE YOUR MONEY MINDSET...**
"Believe it"

Step 2: **CURB YOUR CONSUMERISM...**
"Live a comfortable life, not a wasteful one"

Step 3: **ELIMINATE DEBT...**
"Achieve financial independence"

Step 4: **CREATE A BUDGET...**
"Live within your means...always"

Step 5: **SAVE, SAVE, and SAVE...**
"Make saving a priority"

Step 6: **EDUCATE YOURSELF...**
"Knowledge is key"

FOREWARD

Every day we are learning that individual debt is growing at an astronomical rate and people spend far more than they earn. Foreclosures, bankruptcies and consumer delinquency have reached an all-time high. A major part of the problem has stemmed from the fact that the majority of us were not provided with a financial education program either at home or in our schools.

Unfortunately, financial literacy in our homes and schools was just not a top priority. In fact, The Council for Economic Education has recently noted that only 14 states require students to take a personal finance course in high school. Even more, a recent study found one third of parents are more comfortable talking with their kids about smoking, drugs, and bullying than about money.

But the good news is that **it's not too late**!!

"If I only knew then what I know now" takes you through 6 simple steps that you can use now to manage your money more effectively and achieve the financial independence that you so richly deserve.

It focuses on those key financial skills that are critical now and will continue to play an important role in your journey to achieve personal and financial success.

STEP 1
CHANGE YOUR MONEY MINDSET
"Believe it"

What you think and say to yourself daily about your finances is critically important. In fact, it can bring life or death to your financial situation. I purposely made the topic of mindset step 1 for a reason; your attitudes and psychology around money really do affect how you handle it.

Having a poor mindset can be the reason you end up making all kinds of bad money moves like going deep into debt, not paying bills on time, continuously making expensive purchases, dipping into retirement savings, just to name a few. In order to experience financial independence, we must transform our thought process by deciding to make better financial decisions, rid ourselves of debt, and make deliberate, conscious decisions with money that match our financial goals.

I once told a person close to me that I wanted to live debt free. They replied..."You'll always owe somebody". Wow, what a profound statement I thought, is that true? Will I never be able to experience financial independence because no matter what I do, I'll "*always owe somebody*?"

I could have accepted what they told me and continued to live in financial mediocrity. I probably would have still been able to live a comfortable life...barring no major unexpected financial expenses. But, I thought, do I really want to live like that, under such financial uncertainties? Absolutely not!

At that very moment, I decided that I CAN and WILL achieve financial independence.

What you believe about your ability to effectively manage your money and experience financial independence for yourself determines your success. When you change your mindset and truly believe in your ability to transform your financial situation, nothing will be able to stop you.

I encourage you to believe in your ability to achieve financial independence. Regardless of your current financial situation or any future financial challenges that may be on the horizon, know that you can do it. With proper commitment, focus, and planning you can be well on your way to changing your money mindset and achieving the financial freedom that you deserve!

Final Thought

"The only thing that stands between a man and what he wants from life is often merely the will to try and the faith to believe that it is possible."

STEP 2
CURB YOUR CONSUMERISM
"Live a comfortable life, not a wasteful one"

Simply put....stop spending on frivolous items! Obviously, it's not that simple for many of us, since most of us do fall victim to spending, spending, and more spending on things that we really don't need or certainly could live without. Ask yourself, how many pairs of shoes do I really need? Is it really that necessary for me to have that designer dress, or would this less expensive version of the same dress work just as well? Should I have spent my bonus money on that new television, did I really need a new television? Do I shop for items on sale, or am I fine with paying full price for any item..no matter what it is? In answering these questions, be honest with yourself.

My point is not to make you feel bad, but it is to encourage an awakening in your spirit that will help you curb your spending and take control of your financial future. Before you make a purchase, think about the need to purchase that item and the cost. Rather than making that purchase, can you add that money to your savings instead? Before you know it, that small amount of money that you decided to keep and save will accumulate into hundreds, then thousands, and even more!

Now I don't want to take away all of your enjoyment in life. If you work hard, you should be able to spend a little on yourself. But again, it simply goes back to my original point – that is – re-evaluate the way you spend money and think twice before making that purchase.

You can easily save hundreds of dollars a year on clothing purchases by waiting for sales or shopping at discount retailers. Better yet, avoid name brand clothing all together.

Become a wise consumer by comparison shopping, visiting second-hand and thrift shops, or trading children's clothing with friends and relatives. You could even consider putting what you don't need, use and want on eBay or another outlet rather than renting a storage unit to contain all of the purchases you have made that are gathering dust.

If you make small changes in your spending habits and make a conscious decision to curb your consumerism, you will be well on your way to a path of financial independence.

I encourage you to live a comfortable life, not a wasteful one. Do not spend to impress others. Do not live life trying to fool yourself into thinking wealth is measured in material objects. Manage your money wisely, so your money does not manage you.

Final Thought

"One of the best ways to save money is to be content with what you have. Cultivate contentment with yourself and your life, and stop looking for happiness and fulfillment in material things. You'll find that you spend less and save more when you recognize that you have enough."

STEP 3
ELIMINATE DEBT
"Achieve Financial Independence"

So, you now believe that you can achieve financial independence and you've successfully curbed your endless cycle of spending and consuming. Congratulations!! Now what's next?

Now it's time to focus on paying off your debt. Because you curbed your spending and, as a result, have managed to save some cash, you can now use this cash to pay off some (or all) of your debt.

There's an old adage that says *"If you fail to plan, you plan to fail".* This is more than just a clever play on words. In fact, statistically it has been proven that you are more likely to achieve your goals if they are written down. While the importance of planning is most commonly associated with business goals, it most certainly applies to one's financial goals as well.

Your efforts to eliminate debt should always start with developing a plan. You need to know how much your total debt is and how long it will take you to pay it off given your current payment plan. Then begin to eliminate one debt at a time...starting with the smallest first. If all of your debt has similar interest rates or balances, I encourage you to start with the smallest because once you pay this one off, you will be motivated to continue on with your plan.

However, as a point of caution, if you have debt that carries very high interest rates, you should focus on paying this debt first. In this case, what you are aiming to do is eliminate the debt with the highest interest rate first.

As you are paying off your debt, try paying as much as possible each month and always try to pay more than the minimum. Many creditors love it when their clients pay the bare minimum because it means more interest money for them.

By paying only the minimum due each month, you are digging yourself farther into debt. If you want to get out of debt, always pay off as much as you possibly can each month, whether it is the total amount or just a few dollars more than the minimum.

The best way to reduce your debt load is to use some common sense. **The No. 1 reason people have so much debt is because of how easy it is to obtain and use credit.** People fail to realize how much they have already spent, and before they know it, they're maxing out their credit cards on a monthly basis. The best way to know just how much money you are spending is to pay for everything in cash. By paying with cash, you will gain a better appreciation for every hard-earned dollar, and, even more, you will be less inclined to accumulate more debt!

Remember, with patience and commitment you can eliminate your debt once and for all! By following these simple steps you can become debt free faster than you ever thought possible.

Final Thought

"Regardless of how you structure your debt elimination plan, the point is to prioritize and fully understand exactly what you owe. Unless you are crystal-clear about what you owe, it's easy to continue spending money."

STEP 4
CREATE A BUDGET
"Live within your means...always"

The key to any successful financial plan is a solid – and realistic—budget.   While budgeting your money on a daily basis can be an overwhelming process for many, it is vital in keeping your finances on track.   You can use your budget to:

- Assess your financial situation
- Identify your monthly income and expenses
- Set financial goals
- Document expenses
- Commit to a savings plan

Unfortunately, many people balk at the idea of a budget because they do not want to restrict themselves or cut back on their lifestyle and personal priorities. Remember in *"Step 2...Curb Your Consumerism"* we discussed how the desire to have everything often overrules the need to have our finances under control or "on track"? Again, I encourage you not to fall into this trap.   You can create a budget that helps you assess your current financial situation and gain control of your finances, while still allowing for some pleasures in life.

Think of your budget as a plan where you decide at the beginning of the month how much you need to spend on certain things. You know your monthly bills are a priority, so you set money aside to take care of these expenses. You then account for monthly obligations such as food, transportation, day care, or other monthly debt payments.

Finally, allocate a specific amount to go directly to your savings. After these items are taken care of, you can then allocate some money toward (what I call) "pleasure purchases"...whether it's that nice pair of jeans, a night (or two) out on the town, or that latest electronic gadget that's been on your radar. Remember, though, as you are budgeting for your "pleasure purchases", the key is to -- make these purchases in moderation, set spending limits, and always pay in cash.

In creating your budget, it is important to realize that you must provide as much detailed information as possible. Ultimately, you'll be able to see where your money is coming from and where it's going. Here's a simple budget to start you on your way:

Your Monthly Income	Net
Income 1	$
Income 2	$
Other Income	$
Total Monthly Income	$

Your Monthly Expenses	Net
Housing (rent or mortgage plus taxes and insurance)	$
Transportation (car payments, gas, insurance, tolls, etc.)	$
Utilities (Heat, electricity, etc.)	$
Subscriptions (cable, internet, cell phone, gym, etc.)	$
Groceries	$
Medical (co-pays, prescriptions, etc.)	$
Dining, travel, and entertainment	$
Debt payments (credit cards, student loans, etc.)	$
Savings	$
Other discretionary (hobbies, personal care, etc.)	$
Total Monthly Expenses	$

Your Bottom Line	
Income minus expenses	$

Final Thought

"The road to wealth is paved with skillful money management, as well as planning and executing a personal budget."

STEP 5
SAVE, SAVE, and SAVE
"Make Saving A Priority"

If saving money is so important, why is it that most of us don't do it? In fact, there are certainly enough people out there who don't save and spend every dime that they get and they seem to be doing fine, right? So what's the point?

Unfortunately, too many people maintain this way of thinking and don't understand the importance of saving, or better yet, don't make saving a priority. We are conditioned to go out and make as much money as we can and once we do, spend it all and enjoy the fruits of our labor. Of course, I'm not saying you shouldn't enjoy your hard-earned money, but saving money should ALWAYS be a priority.

When you save money you are better prepared for emergencies and are more prepared to take advantage of opportunities that may come your way. This is the importance of saving money.

Interestingly, in talking with people over the years about money issues, I've learned that many of us DO, in fact, want to increase our savings. We recognize that saving money is important, but if you are already struggling to pay bills, it can seem like an impossible ideal. So, how do we save money?

Thankfully, it may not be as difficult as one might think. Saving money is neither a science nor an art; rather it's somewhere in between and requires your commitment and hard work. Here are some techniques that you can use to build your savings:

Set a savings goal

If you do not have a savings account, or are not consistently saving, then setting a goal is key. Start by establishing a realistic savings goal, of course with the understanding that this goal will increase with time. Figure out how much you actually need to save. Many experts agree that you should have at least 6 months of reserves just in case you are out of work. But it can't hurt to be more cautious and save up a year's worth of reserves.

Take a look at your obligations and determine what you can reasonably put away without having to sacrifice too much. Now calculate how much money you need to contribute to your savings account each week, month etc., until you reach your goal. Remember, your goal should be easy to hit without making the act of saving too burdensome.

Automate your savings

One of the simplest and most effective tools you can use for almost any saving goal is an automatic savings plan.

After determining your savings goal, figure out how much money you want to save each time you get paid. Set up an automatic savings program that allows your employer to deduct a certain amount from each paycheck and deposit it into your savings accounts. This way, if you don't see it...you won't miss it.

You can also transfer a pre-determined amount of money from your checking account into your savings account on a regular basis. Either way, these automatic transfers add discipline to your savings. Using a little bit of automation can make the savings process easier and more effective.

Ignore raises, bonuses, and surprises

Oftentimes we receive an unexpected raise, bonus, or just unexpected cash. When this happens, pretend like you didn't get it. Put it directly into your savings account and consider it an increase in your savings.

If you were living comfortably prior to your raise or prior to receiving the unexpected cash, why should this extra cash change your spending habits?

Saving money is within your control

Oftentimes, saving money can seem like such a chore. However, it is necessary in order for one to truly gain control of their finances. I encourage you to make saving a priority today. Saving money is within your control and can bring you huge benefits. By employing the simple techniques outlined in this chapter, you will be well on your way to achieving your savings goals and becoming more financially independent.

Final Thought

"Saving can help you achieve any financial goal. You'll be more likely to save money if you make it a priority."

STEP 6
EDUCATE YOURSELF
"Knowledge is key"

Knowledge is the key to effective money management. If you are truly committed to taking financial control of your life, you must educate yourself on the best strategies for managing, saving, and yes, one day soon, investing your money. The more you learn and know about debt reduction, money management, saving strategies, and building wealth, the more likely you are to achieve your personal finance goals, whatever they may be.

Explore financial resources
As you embark upon your quest for knowledge, I encourage you to continuously explore books (like this one), magazines, newspapers, and the like that focus on money management, debt reduction, and other money related topics.   You can find a wealth of knowledge and resources on personal finance and money management in many of these publications.

Talk to friends *(who are financially successful themselves)*
One of my favorite ways to learn is by talking to friends about money and investing. There are some people out there (hopefully people in your circle of influence) who are financially successful and have

mastered the art of effective money management. Don't be afraid to talk about money with these individuals. I'm sure if you express an interest in knowing how they've become financially successful, they would be more than willing to share their knowledge with you. Actually, I think we would all be better off if we were more open about money issues.

Hire a financial consultant
And, finally, you should always consider meeting with a financial consultant (like myself). Meeting with a financial consultant is a great way to get a better understanding of the best ways to manage your money. This professional will work with you to review your finances, help you develop and set financial goals for yourself, help you implement strategies to ensure you achieve your financial goals, and monitor your progress along the way.

When choosing a financial consultant, look for one who is certified and willing to send you free information about his/her services. Most of all, be sure to choose one that is committed to your financial success and has your best interest in mind.

In order to live a life of truly being good at something, we must not only teach ourselves the basics but also continue to educate ourselves on the topic. Managing our finances is no different.

Final Thought

"Knowledge is the key to successful money management...now and in the future"

"Financial independence means having control over your time without worrying about the ability to pay your bills or forgo experiences you'd like to share with your friends and family."

**Resources**

HOW WELL DO YOU MANAGE YOUR MONEY?

Answer the following questions to assess your financial practices:

I pay the rent/mortgage payment and utility bills on time

   ○   Always   ○   Sometimes   ○   Never

I have a healthy savings account

   ○   Always   ○   Sometimes   ○   Never

I plan ahead for large expenses, such as taxes and insurance

   ○   Always   ○   Sometimes   ○   Never

I set goals and have a spending plan for my net income

   ○   Always   ○   Sometimes   ○   Never

I use my credit cards wisely

   ○   Always   ○   Sometimes   ○   Never

I comparison shop for the purchases of most items

   ○   Always   ○   Sometimes   ○   Never

I keep track of my daily expenses

   ○   Always   ○   Sometimes   ○   Never

I balance my checkbook regularly

   ○   Always   ○   Sometimes   ○   Never

I check my credit report at least once a year

   ○   Always   ○   Sometimes   ○   Never

SCORING
*Give yourself 2 points for each **Always**; 1 point for each **Sometimes**; and 0 points for **Never***
20-15 You are practicing good money management skills
15-10 You are making an effort to improve your skills
10-0 You need to improve your money management skills

CHOOSING YOUR FINANCIAL GOALS

What are your goals? They are what will motivate you to stay on track with your spending plan. Without goals, you may find yourself living paycheck to paycheck and never saving for those things you really want.

You will probably have short- and long-term goals. Every family member should take part in selecting them. Consider these goals when developing your spending plan.

SHORT-TERM GOALS (WITHIN ONE YEAR)

1._____

2._____

3._____

4._____

LONG-TERM GOALS (MORE THAN ONE YEAR)

1._____

2._____

3._____

4._____

EXAMPLES:
Short-Term Goals *(within one year)*
- Pay off credit card bill
- Save for family vacation

Long-Term Goals *(more than one year)*
- Purchase a car
- Save for retirement

DEBT REPAYMENT – GOAL CHART

Creating a debt goal chart can give your debt repayment some structure and help you monitor the progress you are making each month. Consider using the chart below:

Creditor	Balance	Interest Rate	Current Monthly Payment	Goal Monthly Payment	Pay Off Date (based on Goal Monthly Payment)

Tips:
- ✓ Treat yourself to a small reward every time you reach a milestone in your debt payoff

- ✓ Go over your budget periodically to look for areas where you can cut spending. Allocate any extra money toward paying off existing debt

27

OBTAINING YOUR CREDIT REPORT AND SCORE

Check your credit report and score at least twice year to review your payment history and ensure all information on your report is accurate.

To obtain your credit report and score, you should check the three credit reporting companies for the best price. The three credit bureaus are:

Equifax (www.equifax.com or 1-800-685-1111)
Experian (www.experian.com or 1-888-397-3742)
Trans Union (www.transunion.com or 1-800-916-8800)

You will need to provide your full name, including any maiden name; current address; previous address; Social Security number; and date of birth.

If you are applying for a loan, check your credit score to learn if lenders consider you a good credit risk. Credit scores are usually between 300 and 850. Five factors determine credit scores:

- ✓ Payment history
- ✓ Amount of Debt
- ✓ Credit account history
- ✓ Recent credit history
- ✓ Types of credit you have

As a point of caution, with the increasing amount of identity theft, it is to your benefit to guard your personal information carefully and check your credit report regularly.

Please note, legitimate consumer reporting companies will not call you or send an email asking for personal information. On the Web, do not open emails or click pop-ups that offer a free credit report. You cannot obtain a free credit report by contacting a consumer reporting company directly.